WELCOME TO THE WORLD OF ANIMALS

Hummingbirds

Diane Swanson

Gareth Stevens Publishing
A WORLD ALMANAC EDUCATION GROUP COMPANY

Please visit our web site at: www.garethstevens.com
For a free color catalog describing Gareth Stevens Publishing's list of high-quality books and multimedia programs, call 1-800-542-2595 (USA) or 1-800-387-3178 (Canada). Gareth Stevens Publishing's fax: (414) 332-3567.

The publishers acknowledge the support of the Canada Council for the Arts and the Cultural Services Branch of the Government of British Columbia in making this publication possible.

Library of Congress Cataloging-in-Publication Data

Swanson, Diane, 1944-
    Hummingbirds / by Diane Swanson.
       p. cm. — (Welcome to the world of animals)
    Includes index.
    Summary: Describes the physical characteristics, behaviors, and habitat of hummingbirds.
    ISBN 0-8368-4024-0 (lib. bdg.)
    1. Hummingbirds—Juvenile literature. [1. Hummingbirds.] I. Title.
    QL696.A558S83   2004
    598.7'64—dc22   2003060376

This edition first published in 2004 by
Gareth Stevens Publishing
A World Almanac Education Group Company
330 West Olive Street, Suite 100
Milwaukee, WI 53212 USA

This U.S. edition © 2004 by Gareth Stevens, Inc. Original edition © 2002 by Diane Swanson. First published in 2002 by Whitecap Books, Vancouver. Additional end matter © 2004 by Gareth Stevens, Inc.

Series editor: Betsy Rasmussen
Design: Melissa Valuch
Cover design: Steve Penner

Cover photograph: Anthony Mercieca/Dembinsky Photo Assoc.
Photo credits: Alan G. Nelson/Dembinsky Photo Assoc. 4; Anthony Mercieca/Dembinsky Photo Assoc. 6, 14, 16, 26, 28; Rob and Ann Simpson 8, 10, 18, 20, 22, 24, 30; Dominique Braud/Dembinsky Photo Assoc. 12

Printed in the United States of America

1 2 3 4 5 6 7 8 9 08 07 06 05 04

Contents

World of Difference

Hummmm . . . Hummmm . . . Hummmm. It is much easier to hear hummingbird wings than it is to see them. They beat so fast they blur. But they are just what a hummingbird needs to dart around fields, dipping its beak into flowers to dine.

English-speaking people named hummingbirds after the hum of their beating wings, but people who spoke Portuguese focused on the way the birds feed. Their word for hummingbird means "kiss the flower." The French seemed especially struck by a hummingbird's little body, naming it "fly-sized bird."

Of all the birds in North America, the calliope hummingbird is the littlest.

5

A blue-throated hummingbird shines in the light.

Hummingbirds are the smallest birds in the world. The calliope hummingbird is the tiniest in North America. Fully grown, it is as short as your thumb and weighs less than a penny.

The calliope is one of approximately 340 different kinds of hummingbirds. North America, including Mexico, is home to about fifty kinds.

All hummingbirds have thick coats. For their size, they produce more feathers than any other bird. And on many hummingbirds, some of those feathers gleam like colorful jewels in bright sunshine. Stand between a hummingbird and the Sun— with the light to your back— and you will witness the flash as the bird faces the Sun. WOW! But when the light or the angle is not right, the brilliance disappears, and bright colors fade to drab.

Hats Off to Hummingbirds

Here are some hummingbird facts.

· Three broad-tailed hummingbird chicks— newly hatched—weigh only as much as a single paper clip.

· One blue-throated hummingbird nest, used for ten years, contained 15,000 miles (24,000 kilometers) of spider silk.

· Some hummingbirds carry hitchhikers. Mites catch rides in the birds' nostrils, then race down their beaks to feed on flowers.

Where in the World

Hummingbirds live where flowers bloom—but only in the western half of the world. Hummingbirds live in North, Central, and South America. Most kinds live in hot jungles. Others do well in cooler climates. Rufous hummingbirds, for example, spend part of each year in Alaska.

Different hummingbirds live in different types of homes—along sea coasts, in forests, in mountain meadows, in deserts, and on grassy plains. Some raise their families in the wilderness, but others raise families in busy city parks and backyard gardens. If you set out a feeder of sugary

A mass of honeysuckle flowers attracts a hungry hummingbird.

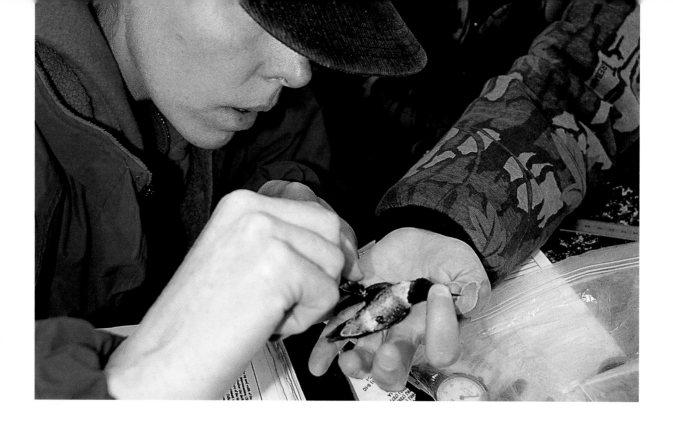

Hummingbirds are banded so researchers can study them more easily.

water, hummingbirds will often arrive for dinner. Some become so comfortable around people, they perch on fingers to eat.

Hummingbirds have territories, areas they defend as their own. Many kinds will challenge an invader head-on. Usually, it is the invader that takes off.

Twice each year, a few kinds of hummingbirds migrate long distances between their summer and winter homes. Ruby-throated and rufous hummingbirds fly more than 2,000 miles (3,200 kilometers) from their nesting sites in the north to their winter homes in the south. About 500 miles (800 kilometers) of the ruby-throated's long journey is across the Gulf of Mexico. It is an amazing trip, which the hummingbirds make nonstop and usually alone.

TAGGED FOR TRACKING

Spot hummingbirds wearing bracelets and you will have found birds tagged by researchers. Scientists are trying to learn more about where hummingbirds travel and how long they live.

Being tagged does not bother the birds. Bands are snapped around their legs. Dates and numbers on the bands are recorded; then the birds are released. One rufous tagged in British Columbia, Canada, turned up in New Mexico six weeks later.

World Full of Food

Imagine eating six times an hour. That is nothing for a hummingbird. When it is not resting, it normally feeds every ten minutes—sometimes more often—eating about sixty meals a day!

Hummingbirds are so active they burn up energy fast. One scientist figured that if an average man used as much energy as a ruby-throated hummingbird, he would need to eat 285 pounds (130 kilograms) of hamburger every day. And before the ruby-throated migrates, it stores energy by eating even more than usual, growing about 50 percent heavier. The extra weight slows its speed, but it helps the bird fly farther.

Feeding from this trumpetlike bloom is no problem for a ruby-throated hummingbird.

13

Tree sap, oozing from holes left by sapsuckers, makes a meal for a rufous hummingbird.

A hummingbird feeds mostly on nectar — the sweet liquid formed inside flowers. The bird sticks its long tongue into a blossom and laps the nectar. The liquid rises through grooves along the bird's tongue. Then the bird draws its tongue back in. Its beak squeezes the nectar off when the bird sticks its tongue out again. To get enough food, a hummingbird might need to visit three thousand blossoms in a single day.

The fringed, split tip of the tongue of many kinds of hummingbirds can pick up meals of insects and spiders along with the nectar. The birds also catch insects in flight and snatch spiders from their webs.

Some kinds, such as ruby-throated and Anna's hummingbirds, feast on sweet tree sap, too. They lunch at holes drilled through the bark by woodpeckers called sapsuckers.

PAYING THEIR WAY

Hummingbirds serve the plants that feed them. When the birds poke their tongues into a blossom, powdery pollen sticks to their heads. That pollen rubs off on the next blossoms the birds visit. Most flowers need pollen from other blooms to produce seeds.

Mountain flowers called paintbrushes depend almost completely on hummingbirds to spread their pollen. The blossoms don't attract insect pollinators because the nectar is too deep for insects to reach.

World in Motion

Walking is not for hummingbirds. Their legs are not built for the job. The birds might shuffle along a branch, but even for short stretches such as that, they are much more likely to fly.

Hummingbirds are most at home in the air. They are champion acrobats of the sky! Not only can they zoom forward like other birds, they can also go backward. As they move from flower to flower, they flit sideways easily. If flying upside down might help hummingbirds escape danger, they can do that, too — for short distances. But most amazingly of all, hummingbirds can hover in midair.

Like other hummingbirds, this Costa's hummingbird rarely uses its tiny legs to travel.

Narrow, pointed wings help make these acrobatics possible. The wings are strong, too. The muscles that move the wings weigh at least one-quarter as much as the whole bird. And the hummingbird moves its wings in an odd way, tracing figure eights in the air. That helps it create power on both the upbeat and

A hummingbird beats its wings too fast to be seen clearly.

18

the downbeat. Depending on the kind of hummingbird and what it is doing, it often beats its wings more than forty times a second!

The hummingbird travels at a quick pace for its size. The ruby-throated humming-bird has been clocked flying at 27 miles (43 kilometers) an hour. It flies — and dives — much faster when it is trying to attract a mate or when it responds to threats. But traveling at full speed does not end in crash landings. A hummingbird can make sudden stops — even on a narrow perch — with grace.

COOL BIRDS

Like you, hummingbirds rest at night. But if the air is cold, day or night, they enter a deep sleep called torpor. Heart and breathing rates drop, and body temperatures fall to just above air temperatures. This deathlike sleep helps the birds survive by saving energy.

The trouble is that hummingbirds cannot escape danger until they come out of torpor. An Anna's hummingbird, for example, cannot fly until its body warms to about 86°F (30°C).

World of Words

Showing off is one way to send signals. During mating seasons, male hummingbirds use fancy flying to tell females they want to mate. Each kind has its own style. Ruby-throated males often sweep back and forth in front of females. Lucifers spiral upward, then plunge straight back down. Black-chinned males perform figure eights, over and over again.

Many hummingbirds deliver these high-flying signals in bright sunshine where their throat feathers "light up." The flashing is another sign of their interest.

A male black-chinned hummingbird displays his colors, attracting the eye of a female.

"Go away!" A female rufous hummingbird tries to scare off a jay.

Some, such as male Costa's, add sound to their showy flights. They dive so fast the air whistles through their feathers. Broad-tailed hummingbirds tri-l-l-l-l when air speeds through slots formed by the narrow tips on a few of their feathers. Some male hummingbirds also sing to their mates by twittering, squeaking, or clicking.

So what is the female response to all this? Anna's hummingbirds express their interest by fluffing up their feathers, wiggling their heads, and squeaking. Then they fly off to the nests they are building — with the males flying after them. White-eared females also lead males to their nesting areas.

Once there, a female might fly from perch to perch, followed by a male. They also take flights together, now and then hovering beak to beak. It is a way of saying, "Let's mate."

GET THE MESSAGE?

Hummingbirds face many dangers. Fish and frogs sometimes grab the birds when they are near water. Nectar-feeding orioles might fight them for flowers. Jays, snakes, and squirrels often eat their eggs or chicks.

Still, as small as they are, hummingbirds use bold body language to scare off many of their enemies. The little birds charge enemies, diving from high above with their spearlike beaks. The message is unmistakable: SCRAM!

23

World of Nests

Hummingbirds can use many things to build their nests, including moss, fungus, blossoms, bark, and even hair and lint from clothes. But there is something else the birds need—silk from spider webs. One of the strongest fibers on Earth, spider silk helps hold the nests together and anchors them firmly in place.

It is the female hummingbirds that build the nests, starting soon after—or just before—they mate. Hovering over the material they have gathered, several kinds of hummingbirds press the nest with their chests, giving it a cuplike shape. Then they

A hummingbird's nest blends well with its surroundings.

Two tiny eggs sit snugly inside a hummingbird's nest.

add linings of soft matter, such as the fluff from dandelion seeds.

The nests vary in size and location, depending on the builder. A ruby-throated hummingbird creates a nest as small as a walnut, while a broad-tailed hummingbird builds one a bit deeper and wider. Tiny calliopes often nest on or near pine cones, making their homes nearly impossible to notice. Blue-throated hummingbirds sometimes find safe nesting spots under bridges, in barns, or on the eaves of houses. Some hummingbirds use a good nest over and over again.

Although Anna's hummingbirds might nest in winter, most hummingbirds wait until spring. Then they lay two white eggs about the size of peas. Within their firm, thick nests, the female birds care for their eggs until they hatch. The birds leave only for short periods to feed.

TOO CLEAN

The folks at the Arizona–Sonora Desert Museum were just trying to improve their live hummingbird display. They hauled out the old plants, enlarged the space, then replanted it. Soon, the birds started nesting again. But the nests they built were too loose. Many collapsed, and the eggs they held fell out.

Museum managers were puzzled until they realized they had cleaned out all the spiders—and the silk webs that hummingbirds need to bind their nests.

New World

A female hummingbird keeps busy on the nest. Using her long beak, she carefully turns her eggs over every few hours. That helps keep them evenly warm as she presses her body against them.

About two weeks after laying her eggs, the hummingbird feels something: tap, tap, tap. The chicks peck away inside their eggs. Hour after hour they work, until finally the shells crack open.

Like many other kinds of birds, hummingbird chicks start life without feathers or sight. It takes a couple of weeks or more before they grow coats and open

Feeding two growing chicks keeps this Anna's hummingbird busy all day.

29

Hummingbirds like this broad-billed hummingbird learn to groom themselves with their beaks.

their eyes. So it is a good thing their mothers look after them. After a mother feeds herself, she returns to the nest and pokes her beak down the throats of the chicks. It looks as if she is hurting the young birds, but she is not. It is her way of pumping some of the food she has eaten directly into the chicks.

When little hummingbirds are only two to three weeks old, they start flying. They are surprisingly good right away, but they have to work to improve their landing skills. Then they can follow their mother from flower to flower and learn to feed as she does. The chicks also practice chasing and catching insects in the air. Sometimes, they chase each other, too — just for fun.

All hummingbird chicks must struggle to survive. If they are lucky, they may live to be five or more years old.

WATER ROMP

If you have ever dashed through the spray of a lawn sprinkler, you know what attracts hummingbirds to hoses. They seem to enjoy the short showers that also keep them clean. Sometimes they dive and roll in the water, riding it as it rises.

At quieter times, hummingbirds bathe in slow-flowing streams —usually in shallow water along the banks. Then they fly to the branches of bushes or trees and shake their feathers dry.

Glossary

hover — to hang fluttering in the air.

invader — an animal who enters into another animal's territory and is not wanted there.

migrate — to move from one region or climate area to another for a season in order to feed or breed.

mites — small animals that travel on or feed on animals

nectar — a sweet liquid produced by flowers.

pollen — a dusty substance on blossoms; it usually needs to be shared with other blossoms in order for plants to produce seeds.

researchers — people who study something carefully in order to learn new things about it.

territories — the areas where animals live, mate, and search for food.

torpor — a slowing down of heart and breathing rates and a lowering of body temperatures to conserve energy.

Index